Fantastic FLOWERS

Written and Illustrated by

Susan Stockdale

PEACHTREE

ATLANTA

Acknowledgments

Special thanks to Dr. Ari Novy of the United States Botanic Garden; Dr. Gary Krupnick of the National Museum of Natural History; and Dr. Peter Zale of Longwood Gardens for their research assistance. They answered many questions regarding my text and illustrations with patience and generosity, and were steadfast cheerleaders to me as I created this book.

Thanks also to Lulu Delacre, Jennifer O'Connell, and Janet Morgan Stoeke for their feedback and support, and for always inspiring me to do my best work.

Flowers in shapes that surprise and delight.

Upside-down pants,

a parrot in flight.

Prim ballerinas,

wild baboons.

Snakes standing guard,

and spiraling spoons.

Heralding trumpets,

a Mexican hat.

Skittering spiders,

a fluttering bat.

Ice cream desserts,

babes taking naps.

Bumblebees laughing,

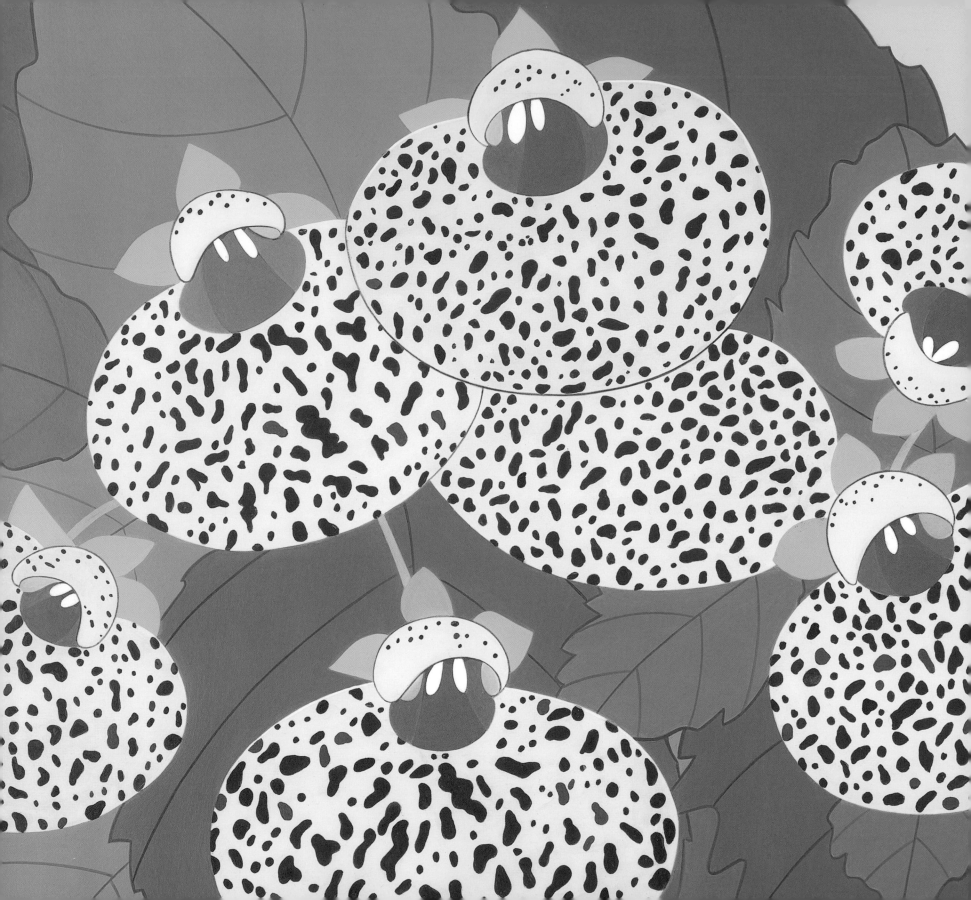

and purses with flaps.

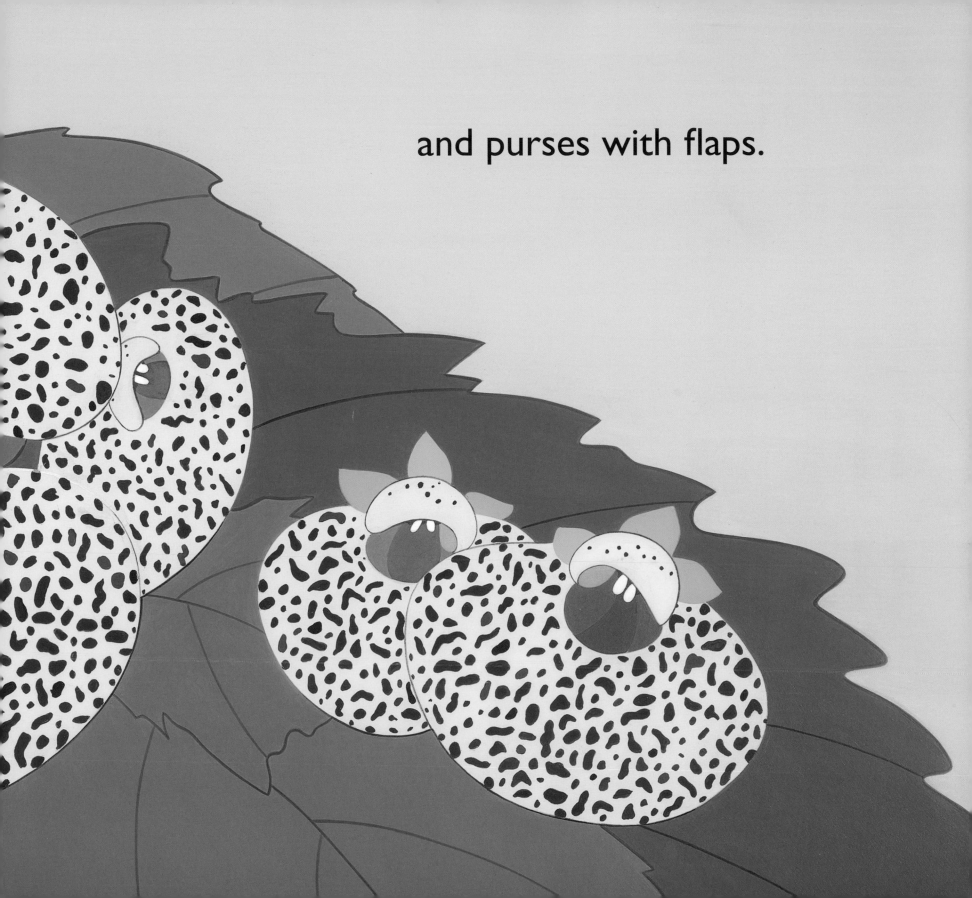

Pineapple posing,

bunches of grapes.

Fantastic flowers

in all kinds of shapes!

A flower is part of a plant. Without flowers, many plants can't reproduce.

Most plants need to be pollinated in order to make seeds for new plants. Pollination occurs when a powder called pollen, created by the male part of the plant (the stamen), reaches tiny egg cells in the female part of the plant (the stigma). As a result, the plant's cells are fertilized and it can produce seeds. Pollination can occur because of the plant's own system, the wind, or by birds, bees, and other animals called pollinators.

When a pollinator visits a flower, pollen sticks to its body. Then when the pollinator visits the next flower of the same type, it leaves behind some of the pollen. Now the second flower has been pollinated and a new seed can grow.

Pollinators are very important. They help produce fruit and seeds for more than one hundred foods we eat, from apples, strawberries, and grapes to broccoli, almonds, and even chocolate. Without pollinators, many plants would become extinct.

A plant may develop in a special way in order to attract a particular pollinator. It may produce special scents or display brilliant colors and unusual shapes to make pollinators notice it. Some flowers have petal and leaf shapes that look like other things, such as a monkey, a hat—even a tiny baby!

Common name:
hot lips

Scientific name:
Psychotria elata

Native range:
Central and South America

Pollinator: hummingbirds, butterflies, moths, and bees

Common name:
ballerina orchid

Scientific name:
Caladenia melanema

Native range: Australia

Pollinator: thynnid wasps

Common name:
Dutchman's breeches

Scientific name:
Dicentra cucullaria

Native range:
North America

Pollinator: bumblebees

Common name:
monkey orchid

Scientific name:
Dracula simia

Native range: Ecuador

Pollinator: fungus gnats

Common name:
parrot flower

Scientific name:
Impatiens psittacina

Native range:
Southeast Asia

Pollinator: unknown

Common name:
friar's cowl

Scientific name:
Arisarum vulgare

Native range: Mediterranean

Pollinator: flies and moths

Common name:
African daisy

Scientific name:
Osteospermum hybrid*

Native range: South Africa

Pollinator: bees,
butterflies, and moths

Common name:
red spider flower

Scientific name:
Grevillea speciosa

Native range: Australia

Pollinator: honey-eating
birds and other birds

Common name:
trumpet creeper

Scientific name:
Campsis radicans

Native range: North America

Pollinator: Ruby-throated
hummingbirds, bumblebees,
and bees

Common name:
black bat flower

Scientific name:
Tacca chantrieri

Native range: Southeast Asia

Pollinator: self-pollinating

Common name:
Mexican hat

Scientific name:
Ratibida columnifera

Native range: North America

Pollinator: bees and
butterflies

Common name:
tulip

Scientific name:
Tulipa hybrid*

Native range:
not considered native
to any region

Pollinator: bees,
butterflies, and moths

Common name:
swaddled baby orchid

Scientific name:
Anguloa uniflora

Native range: South America

Pollinator: orchid bees

Common name:
pineapple lily

Scientific name:
Eucomis bicolor

Native range: South Africa

Pollinator: carrion flies

Common name:
bumblebee orchid

Scientific name:
Ophrys bombyliflora

Native range: Mediterranean

Pollinator: long-horned bees

Common name:
blue grape hyacinth

Scientific name:
Muscari armeniacum

Native range: Eastern
Mediterranean

Pollinator: bees

Common name:
pocketbook flower

Scientific name:
Calceolaria hybrid*

Native range: Central and
South America

Pollinator: oil-collecting bees

* Hybrids are the offspring
of two plants that would
not normally form in the
wild. They are often
formed when humans
artificially pollinate two
separate species.

⏻

PEACHTREE PUBLISHERS
1700 Chattahoochee Avenue NW
Atlanta GA 30318-2112
www.peachtree-online.com

Editor: Kathy Landwehr
Art director: Nicola Simmonds Carmack
Typesetter: Melanie McMahon Ives

The illustrations were created in acrylic on paper.

On the front cover: bumblebee orchid
On the back cover: parrot flower, ballerina orchid, and monkey orchid

Printed in November 2016 by RR Donnelley and Sons in China
10 9 8 7 6 5 4 3 2 1
First edition
ISBN 978-1-56145-952-0

PHOTO CREDITS
Dreamstime
hot lips / *Psychotria elata* (Jennifer Stone), trumpet creeper / *Campsis radicans* (Tairen10), Mexican hat / *Ratibida columnifera* (Dfikar), pocketbook flower / *Calceolaria hybrid* (Jinfeng Zhang), blue grape hyacinths / *Muscari armeniacum* (Ben Schonewille)

Shutterstock
Dutchman's breeches / *Dicentra cucullaria* (Tim Mainiero), parrot flower / *Impatiens psittacina* (Sukpaiboonwat), friar's cowl / *Arisarum vulgare* (McCarthy's PhotoWorks), African daisy / *Osteospermum hybrid* (Shulevskyy Volodymyr), red spider flower / *Grevillea speciosa* (Warittha Praisri), pineapple lily / *Eucomis bicolor* (perlphoto)

Missouri Botanical Garden
ballerina orchid / *Caladenia melanema* (Fabricio Jimenez), monkey orchid / *Dracula simia* (Eerika Schulz), tulip / *Tulipa hybrid* (Russo Sarah), swaddled baby orchid / *Anguloa uniflora* (Zackys Andreas Dwi.L)

Smithsonian Institution
black bat flower / *Tacca chantrieri* (L. E Brothers)

iStock
bumblebee orchid / *Ophrys bombyliflora* (raulbaenacasado)

Library of Congress Cataloging-in-Publication Data

Names: Stockdale, Susan.
Title: Fantastic Flowers / written and illustrated by Susan Stockdale.
Description: Atlanta, GA : Peachtree Publishers, 2017.
Identifiers: LCCN 2016017194 | ISBN 9781561459520
Subjects: LCSH: Flowers—Juvenile literature.
Classification: LCC SB406.5 .S76 2017 | DDC 635.9—dc23 LC record available at
https://lccn.loc.gov/2016017194